Cognitive Learning Strategies for Minority Handicapped Students

Catherine Collier
John J. Hoover

Hamilton Publications
Lindale, Texas

Library of Congress Catalog Card Number: 87-81734

ISBN 0-940059-02-9

Contents

Preface

An increasing number of students from different cultural and linguistic backgrounds, who are enrolled in our public schools, have unique learning needs as they attempt to acquire English as a second language and to adapt to the culture of the American educational system. Among this diverse population of students are learners who have various handicapping conditions. This situation presents even the most experienced teacher with unique challenges as the educational needs of these special learners are addressed. As a result, the classroom teacher must be prepared to deal with a variety of special needs. Numerous strategies exist to assist a teacher to improve the learning environment and interaction in the classroom for culturally and linguistically different students. One important strategy to assist minority students in elementary and secondary school who are handicapped is to address the instructional implications of their different cognitive and learning styles. This book synthesizes information about cognition and learning styles and its implications for cognitive learning strategies instruction for culturally and linguistically different students with learning and behavior problems. This includes minority students who exhibit problems often associated with learning disabilities, mental retardation, or emotional disorders.

This book is divided into three sections. Section I focuses on cognitive learning styles and associated learning style preferences. In this Section, cognitive styles relevant to the education of minority students and particularly minority students who are handicapped are presented. Various learning style preference characteristics associated with the cognitive styles are also discussed. Section II presents coverage of cognitive learning strategies available to and appropriate for use by minority students who are handicapped. The topic of identifying student learning styles is also

addressed in Section II. The final section of this
book discusses strategies for developing and
implementing a program which facilitates student use
of appropriate cognitive learning strategies in
mainstream classrooms. Important factors associated
with regular and special education program
collaboration are explored in Section III.

Although applicable to any learner, the
information on cognition, learning styles, and
cognitive learning strategies presented in this book
apply specifically to minority handicapped students
who have learning and/or behavior problems. This
book was written for practicing teachers who are
faced with the challenge of providing education to
minority students with learning and behavior
problems, although preservice teachers should also
find this book to be an asset as they prepare for
their teaching careers. The authors appreciate the
comments from the professionals who reviewed this
manuscript at various stages of development. Their
thorough reviews and insightful suggestions provided
invaluable assistance in the preparation of this
book.

C.C.
J.J.H.

SECTION I
COGNITION AND LEARNING STYLES

Introduction

Curiosity about how we learn and how we learn to think has existed for centuries. Various philosophers and educators through the ages have developed strategies for enhancing the learning process and for promoting cognitive development. For example, Aristotle developed techniques of association and visual imagery which are still used as mnemonic devices today.

Each of us has our own styles of learning and thinking which differentiate us from others. We also have ways of learning and thinking which we share with others of similar background. We share many similarities with others raised in the same linguistic and cultural environment relative to ways in which we process and use information. This shared cognitive style differentiates us from those raised in different linguistic and cultural environments. Knowledge of these similarities and differences is crucial in education. While accepting that students will interact with and deal with curricular learning experiences in their own individual manners, curriculum development is often based upon our understanding of the shared elements of the learning process.

As Slife, Weiss, and Bell (1985) noted, students who are successful learners spontaneously use cognitive learning strategies when learning new information. Successful learners use cognitive learning strategies selectively to retain information and develop academic skills. The selective use of cognitive learning strategies, especially as these relate to cognitive styles and associated learning styles, is the central focus of this book. Figure 1 summarizes seven pairs of cognitive styles, their associated learning styles, and major cognitive learning strategy clusters that may be used to address specific learning style needs of minority handicapped students. This Figure was developed from several sources including Cawley, 1985; Gardner, 1953; Gardner, Jackson, and Messick,

1960; Mann and Sabatino, 1985; and Ramirez and Castaneda, 1974. It is not the intent that the cognitive learning strategy clusters presented be all inclusive. There are many cognitive learning strategies and others may also be appropriate. However, each of these cognitive learning strategy clusters has been found to be particularly appropriate among minority and minority handicapped students for the selected learning styles in Figure 1. Each of these cognitive style pairs, their associated learning styles, and cognitive learning strategy clusters are discussed in greater detail throughout this book. However, prior to discussing these three areas, several terms will be defined. They include the terms cognition, learning style, culture, and acculturation as used throughout this book.

Cognition

Cognition is the process of perceiving, attending, thinking, remembering, and knowing (Blumenthal, 1977). This is a continuous process which begins before birth and continues throughout life. Some people have more cognitive capacities than others, and some people use less than they are capable of using. Education can affect this ability to develop and use cognitive processes. As Epstein (1978) noted, education can physically alter the brain, increasing the number of dendritic connections and neural activity. There have been several studies of differences in cognitive style and writers agree that the differences in how we conceptually organize our environment result in characteristic ways of learning from our experiences (Gardner et al., 1960; Mann & Sabatino, 1985; Ramirez & Castaneda, 1974).

Cognitive style is the consistent pattern displayed as the individual responds to the environment. Keogh (1973) defined cognitive styles as the stable, typical, and consistent ways in which individuals select and organize environmental data.

3

Figure 1
Cognitive Styles, Associated Learning Styles, and Cognitive Learning Strategy Clusters

COGNITIVE STYLE	ASSOCIATED LEARNING STYLES	COGNITIVE LEARNING STRATEGY CLUSTERS
1. FIELD Independent and Sensitive	Tendency to see everything as elements making up a whole; emphasis upon the parts and not the whole. Tendency to see the whole; difficulty separating the whole from its parts.	Evaluation Organization
2. TOLERANCE High Tolerance and Low Tolerance	Tendency to accept experiences that vary markedly from the ordinary or even from reality or the truth. Tendency to show a preference for conventional ideas and reality.	Analogy Coping Rehearsal
3. TEMPO Reflective and Impulsive	Tendency to take more time and generate more effort to provide appropriate responses. Tendency to give first answer that comes to mind even if frequently wrong or inappropriate.	Active Processing Evaluation Rehearsal

4. CATEGORIZATION

Broad — Tendency to include many items in a category and lessen the risk of leaving something out.

and

Narrow — Tendency to exclude doubtful items and lessen the probability of including something that doesn't belong.

> Analogy
> Evaluation
> Organization

5. PERSISTENCE

High — Tendency to work until the task has been completed; seeks any necessary help.

and

Low — Tendency to short attention; inability to work on a task for any length of time.

> Active Processing
> Coping
> Evaluation

6. ANXIETY

High — Tendency to perform less well when challenged by a difficult task.

and

Low — Tendency to perform better when challenged by a difficult task.

> Coping
> Evaluation

7. LOCUS OF CONTROL

Internal — Tendency to think of oneself as responsible for own behavior.

and

External — Tendency to see circumstances as beyond one's own control; luck or others are seen as responsible for one's behavior.

> Active Processing
> Coping
> Evaluation

She also described cognitive style as a specific pattern and organization of cognitive controls over the learning process, and noted that cognitive styles differ due to preference, accessibility, maturity, task requirements, setting, and instructional program. Cognitive style may be manifested in several ways and has associated learning styles.

Learning Style

Learning style is the characteristic way in which the individual student responds to the instructional environment. While viewed as a consistent pattern of behavior, learning style has been shown to change with age and experience (Keogh, 1977). This author also noted that it seems "likely that most children have a variety of responses at their disposal but that they prefer certain strategies and may overlearn given strategies" (p. 335). As a result, it becomes important to determine whether students have a variety of strategies available and whether they are capable of regulating their response styles to a particular task. Identifying and developing learning strategies in students is not sufficient. They must also be provided the opportunity to develop the capacity and knowledge necessary to use those strategies. In essence, minority handicapped students possess various strategies or styles; however, many of these are ineffective, nonproductive, or inflexible, given the academic tasks they are often asked to perform.

Recent developments in cognitive and learning process research and its application to the education of handicapped students have led an increasing number of researchers to call for de-emphasizing cognitive processing capacity itself in favor of establishing cognitive and learning strategies for using this capacity (Stone & Wertsch, 1984). Researchers have argued that it is more useful to focus on changes in the metacognitive or self-regulative skills that students use when carrying out various activities rather than upon processing alone. Providing students who exhibit learning and behavior problems with strategies which they can use to direct their own behavior is viewed as an effective form of remediation (Palincsar, 1986). Of special concern to educators of minority and minority handicapped students is recent research which suggests that students with learning and behavior problems have difficulties spontaneously using cognitive learning strategies when learning new information (Slife, Weiss, & Bell, 1985). These potential problems may be confounded by cultural influences upon the learner. As a result, when considering cognitive and learning strategies of minority handicapped students, the effects of cultural background upon cognitive development must also be addressed.

Culture

Several decades ago, Goodenough (1957) wrote that "...Culture consists of whatever it is one has to know or believe in order to operate in a manner acceptable to its members" (p. 167). He and other cognitive anthropologists remind us that culture is not a material phenomenon, but rather an organization of factors such as behaviors, values, or emotions. It is the concept of things that a particular people use as models for perceiving, relating, and interpreting their environment. From this perception, culture frames the individual's cognitive view of the world.

The way in which individuals perceive, relate to, and interpret their environment, and the manner in which individuals think about their environment, are shaped by the cultures within which they have been raised. Stated differently, to a great extent a person's cognitive development depends upon one's cultural development. Culture shapes the way we think (cognition), the way we interact (behavior), and the way we transmit knowledge to the next generation (education). Our educational system is founded upon our own culturally-based assumptions about what students should learn, how and where they should learn it, as well as why and when they will need this knowledge. In the multicultural environment of the modern American school it is imperative that we become more sensitive to the cultural bases of cognition and the implications they have for the education of students from different cultural and linguistic backgrounds.

Acculturation

The need to address the effects of <u>acculturation</u> is also an important concern to educators who work with minority handicapped students. Acculturation is the process of adaptation to a new cultural environment through which human beings pass when they move from one cultural milieu into another. One response to acculturation may be <u>assimilation</u>, where the first culture is essentially eliminated from the person's cognitive behavior as the second culture takes its place in all aspects of the person's life. This acculturative response is actually rather rare, as a person more frequently integrates the new cultural patterns within the cognitive and behavioral framework of the first culture. This <u>integration</u> is a more common response to the acculturative process and usually results in better mental health for the person experiencing acculturation (Padilla, 1980).

Some psychological responses to the acculturation experience may manifest themselves as behaviors frequently used as indicators of handicapping conditions. These include confused locus of control, heightened anxiety, poor self-image, codeswitching (i.e., substituting words or phrases from one language to another within the same utterance such as "I see el gato"), or withdrawal (Collier, 1985; Padilla, 1980). Since students who consistently demonstrate these types of behaviors are often referred for special services, it is imperative that teachers who work with minority students who are

experiencing acculturation consider the learners'
responses to the acculturation process prior to
making referrals for special education assessment
and programming. Appropriate placement for these
students may be in cross-cultural counseling or
instructional programs rather than a special
education program.

Cognitive Styles and Associated Learning Styles

The cognitive styles summarized in Figure 1 will
be discussed in more detail in this section along
with the learning styles associated with each.
Cognitive style is used here as a heuristic device
as a basis for understanding learning behaviors and
using cognitive learning strategies. As noted by
Mann and Sabatino (1985), cognitive style is a
"hypothetical construct." Cognition cannot be
observed directly nor can it be heard, touched,
felt, or seen. On the other hand, Mann and Sabatino
also stated that "cognitive constructs....are a
productive source of ideas for use with pupils,
while in some cases suggesting actual ways to help
improve the student's behavior and academic
performances" (p. 11). Within this framework, we
have elected to discuss cognitive styles primarily
to provide the foundation for our description and
exploration of learning styles. Table 1, which was
derived from Cornett (1983), Dyal (1984), and
Ramirez and Castaneda (1974), provides descriptive
words characteristic of learning styles associated
with each cognitive style addressed in this section.
As stated previously, these cognitive and learning
styles are not inclusive. Those most relevant to
minority handicapped students are presented.

Field

Field independence and field sensitivity include
differences in cognitive style often referred to as
analytical versus global. That is, field independent

Table 1
Learning Style Preference Characteristics

Field

Field Independent
Analytical
Separation
Emphasis on parts
Discrimination

Field Sensitive
Global
Integration
Emphasis on whole
Generalization

Tolerance

High Tolerant
Fantasy
Imagination
Individualist
Flexible

Low Tolerant
Reality
Realistic
Conformist
Rigid

Tempo

Reflective
Careful
Takes time to respond
Sequential
Serial

Impulsive
Quick
Responds immediately
Random
Simultaneous

Categorization

Broad Categorizer
Inclusive
Lumper
General
Summarizes

Narrow Categorizer
Exclusive
Splitter
Detailed
Outlines

Persistence

High Persistent
Focuses
Persists
Concentration
Structured

Low Persistent
Scans
Gives up easily
Distraction
Unstructured

Anxiety

High Anxious
Cautious
Does not like pressure
Negative stress response
Finds challenge difficult

Low Anxious
Risk-Taking
Likes/Needs pressure
Positive stress response
Finds challenge motivating

Locus Of Control

Internal
Attributes success to own
efforts
Attributes failure to own lack
of effort
Blames self for circumstances
Accepts personal responsibility
for circumstances

External
Attributes success to luck or
ease of task
Attributes failure to fate,
attitudes of others,
or task difficulty
Blames others for
circumstances
Accepts that circumstances
are due to others' actions

thinkers tend to perceive of things as discrete or separate from their background while field sensitive thinkers tend to be more influenced by context. Field independent learners discriminate and separate ideas into parts. Field sensitive students tend to see the whole and have difficulty separating the whole from its parts. Field sensitive learners internalize and integrate ideas into a whole. One might say that field independent thinkers cannot see the forest for the trees while field sensitive thinkers cannot see the trees for the forest. Field independence or sensitivity has been linked to cultural differences in cognitive styles (Ramirez & Castaneda, 1974).

Ramirez, Castaneda, and Herold (1974) have found that field independence and field sensitivity are affected by acculturation. There has been some speculation that certain cultural groups show a distinct preference for either independence (analytical) or sensitivity (global) in their thinking. It has been shown that as Hispanic students acculturate they tend to become more field independent (Ramirez et al., 1974) in school related tasks. This is not surprising given that the American public school curriculum is primarily visual-auditory and teaches analytical skills to the virtual exclusion of global synthesis. In these situations, the teacher's concern should be to develop sensitivity to the match or mismatch between teaching style and the student's learning style. Besides accommodating this match, teachers can teach explicit learning strategies which enhance student abilities to handle the increasing amounts of field independent instruction to which they are likely to be exposed.

Tolerance

Tolerance refers to a willingness to accept experiences that vary markedly from the ordinary or even from the truth. A student with a low tolerance style usually displays a preference for conventional

11

ideas and an orientation towards reality. High tolerance style reflects a willingness or preference for fantastic or unrealistic experiences. High tolerant students tend to accept experiences that vary greatly from common, everyday reality or the truth. High tolerant learners are imaginative, individualistic, flexible, and open to fantasy. Low tolerant learners are realistic, conformist, rigid, and prefer reality.

High or low tolerance also refers to the ability or inability to accept incongruity. This, of course, is highly dependent upon experience. Culturally different students may respond to imaginary, incongruous, unrealistic material quite differently than may be expected by the teacher. Elementary level teachers and curricula frequently rely on the use of make-believe and "fairy tales" in teaching, and in general, encourage the development and use of a high tolerance cognitive style. However, many cultures encourage the development and use of a low tolerance cognitive style. Members of these cultural groups are discouraged from speculation and socially rewarded for adherence to reality (Collier, 1984). A teacher who wishes to develop higher tolerance levels in class should use cognitive learning strategies which develop the understanding and accepting of the actions of the teacher and benefits of the activity.

Tempo

Aspects of cognitive tempo which pertain to the speed and adequacy of hypothesis formulation and information processing fall along a continuum from reflection through impulsivity. Impulsive learners tend to give the first answer they can think of even if it is frequently wrong or inappropriate. Reflective learners usually pause and take time to consider alternative answers. They are more likely to make appropriate responses (i.e., answers related to the issue or task), although not necessarily always the correct or best responses. Reflective students also tend to generate more effort to provide appropriate answers. Reflective learners are careful, sequential, serial, and take time to respond. Impulsive learners are quick, random, simultaneous, and respond immediately. Similar to field independence and field sensitivity, impulsivity and reflectivity have also been associated with cultural preferences in learning style. In addition, impulsive learners can be taught to use their impulsivity appropriately and to learn to be more reflective as a cognitive learning strategy under their control.

Categorization

Categorization refers to the way in which the learner groups items. Much variation may exist in categorization that is dependent upon the context and previous experiences of the learner. In general, some students will group many items in a category to lessen the risk of leaving something out (broad), while others will exclude doubtful items to lessen the probability of including something that doesn't belong (narrow). Broad categorizers are inclusive and general in their thinking. They tend to summarize and lump ideas together. Narrow categorizers are exclusive and detailed in their thinking as they tend to outline and split ideas apart. Considerable differences may exist between the manner in which students categorize information and the manner in which the teacher desires them to categorize information.

Categorization is particularly important since many learning strategies are based upon this cognitive skill. In several studies detailed in Casson (1981), cultural differences in grouping items frequently exceeded the expectations of the researchers. Although the teacher may give students the general instruction to "put everything together which belongs together," the learner may have many alternatives in categorizing the items. For example, provided an apple, orange, banana, cheddar cheese, red cabbage, squash, and blocks (red, orange, and yellow), the students may sort by color, by shape (e.g., round items and long objects), by dislikes or likes, by usefulness to them, or possibly by type of object (e.g., food and nonfood). As a result, teachers should not assume that all students know exactly what categories they have in mind when instructed to complete these types of tasks.

The teacher can develop cognitive learning strategies which enable students to use their different grouping categories appropriately. The teacher should demonstrate and explain how to determine the type of grouping desired or most useful in the situation, as well as discuss the range of possibilities and benefits of the ability to group appropriately. Knowing that items may be differentiated and described in various ways is a cognitive advantage that bilingual students acquire (Ben-Zeev, 1977; Feldman & Shen, 1971; Ianco-Worral, 1972) when they learn a second language, while continuing to develop cognitive and academic skills in their first language. This cognitive advantage usually helps learners to differentiate and to categorize if the teacher provides them with assistance in using their prior knowledge.

Persistence

Persistence refers to variations in the learner's willingness to work beyond the required time, to withstand discomfort, and to face possible failure. Students with high persistence work until the task is complete and tend to seek any necessary help to complete the task. Students with low persistence usually have a short attention span and display an inability to work on one task for any length of time. This is usually related to problems with attention in general. High persistent learners are focused, concentrated, structured, and determined. Low persistent learners are unstructured, distractible, give up easily, and tend to scan.

Also, some students with learning and behavior

problems will display persistence to an unproductive extreme, (i.e., perseveration upon a given activity or action in inappropriate and sometimes self-destructive ways). Students experiencing acculturation may display a low persistence style as a side effect of culture shock (Adler, 1975). Their teachers will need to address their special learning and behavior needs in comprehensive ways. This includes assisting learners to develop cognitive learning strategies which focus their attention and assist them to cope with new tasks while developing cross-cultural communication abilities.

Anxiety

The level of anxiety and apprehension experienced by a student in a particular learning situation is also a factor in attention. Some learners with low anxiety levels perform better when challenged by a difficult task while students in a highly anxious state (a common side-effect of acculturation) will perform less well under the same conditions. High anxiety learners are cautious, do not like pressure, respond negatively to stress, and have difficulty with challenges. Low anxiety learners are risk-takers, respond well to stress and pressure, and are motivated by challenges.

Students who are easily frustrated or who have a low level of tolerance to frustration also experience difficulties maintaining their attention to a difficult learning situation. This type of situation may also be a factor associated with learned helplessness (i.e., students learn to react to low levels of frustration by saying they cannot do the task and cease to attempt any activity connected with the task). Anxiety and learned helplessness can also be a factor in distractibility. As learners decide that they are helpless in attempting a task, their attention is directed to some other usually less productive activity.

Culturally and linguistically different students

exposed to new stimuli may experience problems with
attention. This is due, to some extent, to their
anxiety about the new item, how it may affect them,
what is expected of them, and the lack of known
relevance to their learning needs. The teacher in
this circumstance must make efforts to introduce the
new elements to the students and "mediate" their
identity and use (Feuerstein, 1979).

Locus Of Control

Locus of control refers to whether students
attribute behavior or achievement to internal or
external factors. For example, if students are
successful on a math lesson, they may attribute
their success to luck, effort, how easy it was, or
possibly the teacher's attitude toward them. Of
primary concern is whether the students think of
themselves as responsible for what happens or
whether they view occurrences as being due to
circumstances beyond their control. Learners with a
tendency towards an internal locus of control
attribute success to their own efforts, attribute
failure to their own lack of effort, accept personal
responsibility for circumstances, and blame
themselves for circumstances. Learners with a
tendency to an external locus of control attribute
failure to fate, the attitude of others, or task
difficulty; blame others for circumstances; and,
believe that circumstances are due to others'
actions. Locus of control is an element in cognitive
style as well as being a factor in the successful
use of cognitive learning strategies
(Dudley-Marling, Sinder, & Tarver, 1982; Dyal,
1984). It has also been shown to be an element in
the acculturation process. Students who are
experiencing acculturation have been found to have
confusion in locus of control (Adler, 1975; Juffer,
1983; Padilla, 1980).

Throughout this section several cognitive styles
have been presented. As stated at the beginning of

these discussions, these cognitive styles were presented to provide a foundation for exploring learning styles as well as the appropriate student use of cognitive learning strategies. Section II provides additional discussions about learning styles and detailed discussions about cognitive learning strategies.

SECTION II
COGNITIVE LEARNING STRATEGIES IN THE CLASSROOM

The cognitive learning strategies and techniques described in this section have all been used successfully by the authors with minority students with learning and behavior problems. They have also been used successfully with other students as noted in the research cited for each individual strategy. When modifications for cultural and linguistic concerns are made, these strategies should enhance the classroom teacher's teaching repertoire and assist in improving instruction for minority handicapped students. As noted in Section I, these strategies are not intended to be all-inclusive. There are many cognitive learning strategies; however, the clusters of strategies selected for detailed discussion are those most frequently found to be effective with students with learning and behavior problems, especially those from different cultural and linguistic backgrounds.

In order to select appropriate cognitive learning strategies for particular students, the teacher must initially identify the student's learning style. Although the cognitive styles discussed in Section I are useful for understanding the cognitive base of associated learning styles, the student's learning style is of primary importance to the classroom teacher. We will first discuss the process of identifying learning style and will then provide a detailed description of the clusters of cognitive learning strategies which can be used to address learning style needs.

Identifying Learning Styles

There exist many ways to identify preferences in learning style and a variety of commercial instruments are available to measure various aspects of learning style. However, many of these are time-consuming and may require special training for administration and interpretation. As a result, informal assessment of students' learning styles may be more practical and useful to teachers of minority handicapped students. The informal assessment of learning styles should include the use of informal scales as well as information gathered from teacher observations and student interviews.

The information in Table 2 provides a guide for identifying students' learning style preferences based upon the characteristic behaviors detailed in the previous section. The seven selected cognitive styles which are associated with the learning style preferences are used to categorize the behaviors characteristic of each style. These characteristic behaviors are presented along a continuum. A teacher should rate a particular student's behavior along the continuum. This is easily accomplished by placing an X on each line nearest the descriptor that is characteristic of the student's learning style preference. Once the rating has been completed for each descriptor, through visual examination of the completed guide the teacher obtains a general summary of the student's learning preferences relative to each cognitive style. This information is considered along with data obtained through student interviews and teacher observations of the student's learning preferences.

An additional benefit of student interviews (i.e., asking the students how, when, what, and where they learn best) is that the students become more actively involved in and aware of their own learning processes. The open discussion of effective and ineffective cognitive learning strategies has been shown to be an important element in the retention, transferability, and utilization of strategies (Kurtz & Borkowski, 1984). One technique to obtain student information and to develop learning style awareness is to have students write or orally respond to a productive or non-productive learning situation. Through discussions with the students, an increased awareness of particular learning styles may emerge and in turn assist in the students' overall learning. If students have difficulty using themselves as examples, a fictitious case could be presented. Consider the following example:

Table 2
Guide for Identifying Student Learning Style Preferences

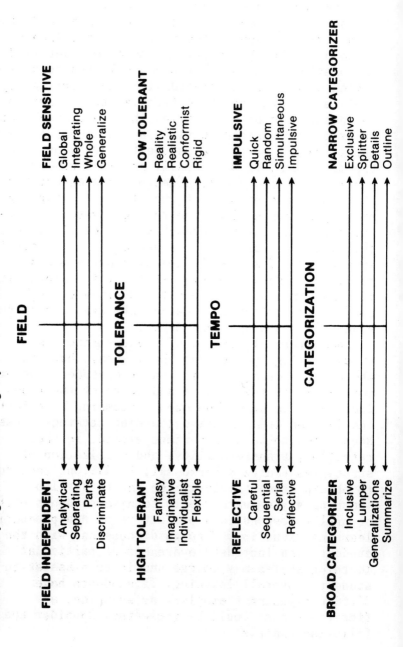

FIELD

FIELD INDEPENDENT | FIELD SENSITIVE
Analytical | Global
Separating | Integrating
Parts | Whole
Discriminate | Generalize

TOLERANCE

HIGH TOLERANT | LOW TOLERANT
Fantasy | Reality
Imaginative | Realistic
Individualist | Conformist
Flexible | Rigid

TEMPO

REFLECTIVE | IMPULSIVE
Careful | Quick
Sequential | Random
Serial | Simultaneous
Reflective | Impulsive

CATEGORIZATION

BROAD CATEGORIZER | NARROW CATEGORIZER
Inclusive | Exclusive
Lumper | Splitter
Generalizations | Details
Summarize | Outline

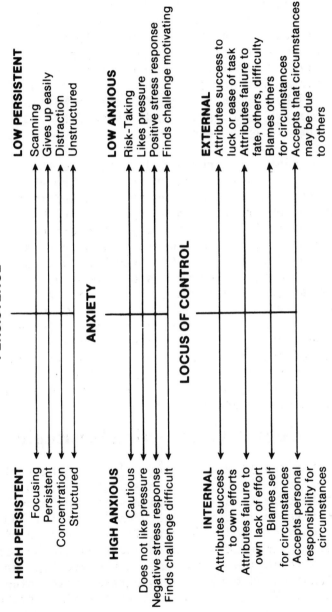

PERSISTENCE

HIGH PERSISTENT
Focusing
Persistent
Concentration
Structured

LOW PERSISTENT
Scanning
Gives up easily
Distraction
Unstructured

ANXIETY

HIGH ANXIOUS
Cautious
Does not like pressure
Negative stress response
Finds challenge difficult

LOW ANXIOUS
Risk-Taking
Likes pressure
Positive stress response
Finds challenge motivating

LOCUS OF CONTROL

INTERNAL
Attributes success to own efforts
Attributes failure to own lack of effort
Blames self for circumstances
Accepts personal responsibility for circumstances

EXTERNAL
Attributes success to luck or ease of task
Attributes failure to fate, others, difficulty
Blames others for circumstances
Accepts that circumstances may be due to others

23

Maria is preparing for a math test. At her school in Mexico, she learned the required level of math calculation to complete the test. However, now she must complete the tasks in English when presented in story problem form. To prepare for the test, Maria spent much time reviewing her multiplication tables aloud and on flash cards. She also had her brother say problems to her in Spanish and practiced responding to them in both languages.

The students are instructed to analyze this situation from their perspectives. Through their analyses, the students should be guided so they are able to compare their own approaches to Maria's, describe Maria's learning style preferences, predict where she might have trouble on the test, and what she should do the next time she has to prepare for a similar test. The teacher should also use information gathered through observations of the students when assisting them to become more aware of their own learning preferences. Data gathered through use of informal scales, teacher observations, and student interviews will provide valuable information to assist in the decision-making process concerning the education of a particular student.

Cognitive Learning Strategies

After identifying a student's learning style preference, the teacher can select clusters of cognitive learning strategies which may prove effective in meeting the student's special learning and behavior needs. To maximize the effects of strategy instruction, the student should be provided with information on the use of the strategy as well as feedback on monitoring progress while using the strategy. The goal of cognitive learning strategies is to increase student control over and use of strategies which increase the capacity for learning. When teaching these strategies in the classroom, it is extremely important to remember that both acquisition of and control over the strategy must be learned. The most effective instructional results have been found when the utility of and the rationale for the strategy are taught along with the technique itself. Kurtz and Borkowski (1984) pointed out that providing students with feedback on the efficacy of the strategy and the long range value of the strategy improves performance and increases the likelihood of the strategy being transferred to other tasks.

Various procedures for teaching one or more cognitive learning strategies have been identified and may vary depending upon the student and the strategy in question (Alley & Deshler, 1979; Gearheart, DeRuiter, & Sileo, 1986; Sheinker & Sheinker, 1983). However, the following instructional steps provide a general structure for teaching cognitive learning strategies:

Step 1: Inform students what the strategy is, how it operates, when to use it, and why it is useful;

Step 2: Use metaphors, analogies, or other means of elaborating on a description of the strategy combined with visual cues;

Step 3: Lead group discussions about the use of the strategy;

Step 4: Provide guided practice in applying the strategy to particular tasks;

Step 5: Provide feedback on monitoring use and success of the strategy; and,

Step 6: Provide generalization activities.

Metacognitive skill development in conjunction with teaching various learning strategies has been shown to be a critical element in the successful utilization and maintenance of cognitive learning strategies by students with learning and behavior problems (Kurtz & Borkowski, 1984).

The information in Table 3 outlines the individual strategies associated with each cluster discussed in this section. Also included in the Table are some desired outcomes when using the strategies, as well as special considerations when using these cognitive learning strategies with minority handicapped students. Table 3 was developed from sources cited in the following discussion, and the reader is referred to those references for additional information about each cognitive learning strategy cluster.

The following discussion details these strategies and provides suggestions concerning how to effectively teach these to minority handicapped students. An application of the strategy follows the discussion about each strategy. Each "Applying the Strategy" section provides an example of the proper use of the strategy from both the teacher and student perspectives. The "teacher" element of each example describes verbal statements or questions made by the teacher to the student. The "student" statements or questions represent examples of student internal, self-talk relative to the "teacher" questions or statements. As the students respond to the teacher's discourse through self-generated questions and statements (and associated responses), they are engaged in the use of the cognitive learning strategy. These examples of application are designed to be general in nature and can easily be applied to most learning situations as student needs and abilities are addressed. The specific language used by the teacher and student illustrated in each example should be simplified, as necessary, to accommodate individual student language proficiency levels.

Active Processing

Numerous studies have been completed which demonstrate effective cognitive strategies for enhancing comprehension, particularly in the area of reading. In general these all use active processing and schema strategies. Within these strategies, the student is induced to generate questions about the subject which activate prior knowledge (schema) or which provide elaboration upon the subject (active processing) (Wong, 1985). The use of self-questioning and speech-to-self or self-talk are important strategic elements in Active Processing. An additional advantage of teaching these strategies to culturally and linguistically different students is that it can enhance language development in the first language and their acquisition of English.

The basic process is one of scanning and summarizing, generating questions about, clarifying important elements of, and predicting or elaborating upon the information to be learned. For example, Wong and Jones (1982) wrote that text comprehension was increased when students learned to use the following strategic sequence:

1) Find and underline the main idea;

2) Think of questions about the main idea;

3) Learn the answer to the generated questions; and,

4) Review these questions and answers to evaluate the information they provide.

Schumaker, Deshler, Alley, Warner, and Denton (1984) used another version of this strategic sequence leading up to self-questioning: survey the materials for the main idea and the organization of the material; read the questions at the end of the chapter to determine what facts are important to learn; and, read the materials and identify key

Table 3
Cognitive Learning Strategies

COGNITIVE LEARNING STRATEGY	DESIRED OUTCOMES	SPECIAL CONSIDERATIONS
ACTIVE PROCESSING Self-Talk Self-Question Self-Reinforce	Language development Access prior knowledge Elaboration Awareness of learning process Develop reflective tempo Reduce low persistence behaviors Reduce confusion in locus of control	If students are very limited English proficient, this should be initiated in L1 with bilingual peer, aide, or teacher assistance. As the students become more proficient and comfortable/familiar with the process, they can do this more often in English.
ANALOGY Rhyme Schema Metaphor	Develop higher tolerance for new/unusual Access prior knowledge Elaboration Build C1-C2/L1-L2 transfer skills Develop categorization skills	Teachers should take some time prior to use of these strategies to acquaint themselves with the culture, language, and experience background of their students. Complete knowledge is not necessary but basic information and sensitivity is crucial. This knowledge will allow the teachers to provide a few examples from the students' backgrounds as an introduction to the strategy.
COPING Confront Engage Solve Ask for aid Implement Persist Outcome/Solution	Problem-solving Awareness of learning process Develop higher tolerance for new/unusual Build self-esteem Develop higher persistence skills Lower anxiety levels Reduce confusion in locus of control	This can be done individually or with groups of students. It is particularly useful in groups for Native American, Asian, and other cultures which use and value group process more than individual achievement. The teacher must be sensitive to cultural differences in problem-solving and use these in comparison.

EVALUATION

Self-Monitor
Check
Reflect
Transfer

Awareness of learning process
Guidelines for selecting/using strategies
Develop field sensitive skills
Develop/utilize field independent skills
Develop reflective tempo
Develop categorization skills
Develop higher persistence strategies
Lower anxiety level
Reduce confusion in locus of control

It is important to demonstrate how to do these skills as well as their importance as cognitive learning strategies. Demonstrate how to check answers and how to transfer these to other activities. Role play, self-monitoring, and reflection can be used to assist in the development of this strategy.

ORGANIZATION

Group
Cluster
Label

Develop association skills
Improve mnemonic retrieval
Develop analytical skills
Cognitive development
Develop field independent skills
Develop field sensitive skills
Develop categorization skills

Teachers should determine what types of categorization the students are using and use these current skills and knowledge as a foundation. Examples from the students' cultures can be used effectively and elaborated upon.

REHEARSAL

Review
Recite
Recall

Improve mnemonic retrieval
Language development
Improve retention of information
Develop higher tolerance for new/unusual
Utilize familiarity (low tolerance style)
Develop reflective tempo

Teachers need to demonstrate how to do this. Role play and acting out can be used to demonstrate rehearsal procedures. This can also be done bilingually (i.e., information in English can be reviewed/recalled in the native language and vice versa).

29

content about which to generate questions. The well-known SQ3R strategy (Survey, Question, Read, Recite, Review) is another application of this active processing strategy.

When teaching these active processing and schema strategies to culturally and linguistically different students, it is important to include explicit cross-cultural assistance. Students will have difficulty comprehending information if they possess no schema (i.e., concepts of phenomena they have previously encountered) for material presented or if their schema differ from that held by the presenter of the material. Delpit (1986) provided an example of a teacher in an Eskimo village who was frustrated during a basal reading lesson. Her students did not understand the meaning of a story because they were not familiar with the word "alley." The students looked up the word in the dictionary and reread the lesson. However, they were still unable to understand the point of the story. Further analysis of the situation and the word "alley" provides insight into these students' potential problems with this reading selection. Think for a moment about all that comes to mind when you hear the word "alley." If you are like most urban Americans you will be thinking about factors such as garbage, danger, murder, rats, or darkness. The lack of such cultural schemata, not included in dictionary definitions, will contribute to the comprehension problems of culturally different students.

Self-talk and self-questioning are also important elements in active processing cognitive learning strategies. Miller (1985) showed that having students talk aloud to themselves while following a learning sequence enhanced their ability to successfully complete a particular task. Other researchers have also provided examples of the proper use of self-talk techniques (Gearheart et al., 1986; Meichenbaum & Goodman, 1971).

Active Processing - Applying the Strategy...

Step 1: <u>Definition</u>

> Teacher–"First, you need to think about what you intend to accomplish in this task. What is it you plan to do? What is your goal?"

> Student–"First, I need to make sure that I know what I am going to do."

Step 2: <u>Specification</u>

> Teacher–"Second, you need to decide what you will need to do to accomplish the task or goal."

> Student–"Next, I need to decide what to do to reach my goal."

Step 3: <u>Evaluation</u>

> Teacher–"Third, you must check what you have done. Has your action provided the correct answer?"

> Student–"I must check my work. Is there anything wrong with my answer or method?"

Step 4: <u>Monitor</u>

> Teacher–"There are usually several ways to accomplish a goal. Also, remember that it is okay to make mistakes as we can learn from our mistakes. Be sure to try another approach if the one you have tried does not appear to work."

Student-"I know that more than one way
usually exists to achieve a goal. I
also know that mistakes can help me
to learn. I will try another
approach if the one I select does
not work."

Step 5: Completion

Teacher-"Finally, you need to recognize
when you have completed the task or
achieved your goal. Remember what
you set out to do and to
congratulate yourself when you have
completed it."

Student-"Did I complete my task? Did
I achieve what I set out to do?
When the task has been completed,
I will congratulate myself for a
job well done."

Analogy

Analogy strategies are another useful means of
enhancing acquisition and retention of new
materials. In analogy, the learner recalls
previously experienced patterns which are similar to
the new items. Englert, Hiebert, and Stewart (1985)
used this strategy to improve the spelling skills of
students with learning and behavior problems. The
students were instructed to identify a previously
known word which rhymed with the new word. They then
identified portions of both words which were spelled
the same. They spelled the new word using the
rhyming elements of the previous word. Students were
then provided the opportunity to apply this by
completing cloze sentences which required the use of
transfer words which rhymed with common words.
Analogy is also a very effective elaboration of

schema (prior knowledge) especially for culturally and linguistically different students. Teachers can encourage minority students to find analogies between new concepts, materials, experiences, or concepts the students have from their home culture or nation of origin. This is a good technique for language development and language transition as well. This use of analogy can be as simple as identifying similar sounds, similar words or cognates, or as complex as discussing similarities and differences in perceptions, values, or abstract concepts. For example, an appropriate economics lesson using analogy strategies would be to discuss how the cultures of the students in the classroom have met the basic needs of food, clothing, shelter, and their exchange systems. Comparisons can be drawn between cultures as similarities and differences are noted. Analogies can be made between these and various social groups in the United States. On a simpler level, younger students could make analogies between letters and sounds in their native language and English.

Analogy - Applying the Strategy...

Step 1: <u>Prior Knowledge</u>

> Teacher-"Can you recall something from your own language or experiences which is similar to this item?"

> Student-"What do I know that is like this item? Is there something in my background, language, or experiences which is similar to the item?"

Step 2: <u>Comparison</u>

> Teacher-"Now examine how these items are similar or different. Do they have similar uses?"

Student–"How are these items similar and
         different? Are they used in similar
         ways?"

Step 3: <u>Substitution</u>

Teacher–"Identify the items or parts of
         items that might be substituted for
         these items. Why would this
         substitution work? Why might it not
         work?"

Student–"Can I use these similar elements
         interchangeably? What other items
         might be substituted for these
         items?"

Step 4: <u>Elaboration</u>

Teacher–"Think about other experiences,
         words, or actions from your life,
         language, or culture which are
         similar to elements of English or
         your life here in this community.
         In what ways are they similar and
         different? How could you use your
         prior knowledge effectively in new
         situations?"

Student–"When the teacher asks for examples
         I can provide them based upon my
         own experiences and do not have to
         use American examples. I know that
         aspects of a new situation may be
         similar to something I know from my
         previous experiences."

Coping

Another problem-solving strategy is the coping sequence recommended by Peck, Hughes, Breeding, and Payne (1980). The advantage of this is that it can be used to assist students from different cultural or linguistic backgrounds to deal with non-academic as well as academic aspects of the learning situation. In addition, this strategy has been found to be effective in cross-cultural situations. The students are taught to confront the problem substantively and not emotionally; engage and initiate action; conceive of a possible solution; request and use assistance; implement their solution; persist in confronting the problem; attempt alternative solutions if the first does not work; and, achieve an outcome.

For example, a group of Indochinese refugee students may feel that the English language lesson they have been given is too difficult. They may also believe that the school is deliberately giving them tasks beyond their capacity. A teacher or counselor who is assisting these students in their acculturation should provide training in coping strategies. The students should be guided so they are able to analyze their language lesson, break it into subtasks, and remind one another not to get emotional about the task. They may also ask different members of their group to work on the different subtasks appropriate to their English proficiency levels. Some members of the group could also be given the task of asking questions and getting answers from the teacher or other students. The next stages in the coping strategy include attempting a solution, persisting in the activity, and attempting various alternatives to deal with different situations. This particular example may also be completed as an individual rather than group task.

Coping - Applying the Strategy...

Step 1: <u>Confrontation</u>

> Teacher-"What are the essential elements of the problem? Have you controlled your feelings about the problem or consequences to the problem?"

> Student-"Can I break the problem into several parts? What can I say about this problem? Have I controlled my feelings relative to the problem?"

Step 2: <u>Plan Strategy</u>

> Teacher-"Break the problem into parts and prioritize them in the order that each should be addressed. Develop a plan for addressing the problem in a step by step manner. Imagine what the solution or answer might be. How will you know that you have resolved the problem?"

> Student-"What are the elements of this problem that must be addressed? In what order should I address the elements? What might possible solutions look like? How will I know that I have resolved the problem?"

Step 3: <u>Assistance</u>

> Teacher-"Study the elements of the problem. Do you need assistance with any of them? Where might you go to find necessary assistance? Everyone

needs assistance from time to time. You must recognize when you need assistance and know how to go about finding necessary help."

Student—"Do I need assistance with any parts of this problem? I know that it is okay to ask for help. Do I know someone who can help me? Do I know how to get necessary help?"

Step 4: Implementation

Teacher—"After you have analyzed your problem and come up with a plan for taking action, you must implement that plan. Knowing that you are initiating your plan is important to coping with problems and situations. You may use a gesture or word to signal that you have begun your plan."

Student—"When I am ready to begin addressing my problem I will snap my fingers or nod my head. I will know that I am ready to begin when I have my action plan ready and have identified potential sources of assistance."

Step 5: Persistence

Teacher—"There are usually several ways to achieve something or solve a problem. Some ways may be more effective than others in different circumstances. Do not stop trying if you have difficulty or meet resistance to solving the problem. Sometimes you must try another approach to achieve a solution.

37

Think of other times when you had difficulty reaching a solution and what you did to resolve that problem."

Student—"I will not stop if I meet with difficulty or resistance. I will attempt different solutions to the problem until the problem has been resolved."

Step 6: <u>Resolution</u>

Teacher—"Part of coping with problems is to recognize that a solution has been reached and that the problem has been resolved. Recall what it was you were attempting to accomplish and what you imagined the solution to be like. When you reach this accomplishment and have a solution that addresses the problem then you can say to yourself that you have resolved this problem. Congratulate yourself for coping with and solving your own problem."

Student—"I have addressed my problem, developed and implemented a plan of action, modified the plan as necessary, asked for necessary assistance, and generated an appropriate solution. I was able to resolve my problem because I am able to ask for assistance when I need it. The solution that I have reached resolves my problem. I congratulate myself for solving my own problem."

Evaluation

Palincsar and Brown (1987) noted that to identify and use appropriate strategies students must learn to evaluate the learning situation. The skills necessary for an evaluative cognitive learning strategy are: "predicting, checking, monitoring, reality testing and coordination, and control of deliberate attempts to study, learn, or solve problems" (Brown, 1980, p. 454).

The teacher's goals in developing the student's evaluation strategy skills include increasing the student's awareness of what he or she needs to do to complete a given task, providing the student with concrete guidelines for selecting and using appropriate specific strategies for achievement, and guiding the student in comprehensive monitoring of the application of the strategy. These goals are accomplished through modeling, demonstrating, and describing the purpose or rationale for using the strategy. This, in turn, assists students to become aware of: the types of tasks or situations where the strategy is most appropriate; the range of applications and transferability; the anticipated benefits from consistent use; and, the amount of effort needed to successfully deploy the strategy (Pressley, Borkowski, & O'Sullivan 1984).

The process of instruction to enhance this cognitive learning strategy described by Palincsar and Brown (1987) and others may be summarized as follows:

1) Careful analysis of the task;

2) Identification of the strategy which will promote successful task completion;

3) Explicit instruction of the strategy and its application to given tasks;

4) Provision of feedback in regard to usefulness of the strategy;

5) Provision of feedback about the success of acquisition of the strategy; and,

6) Assistance in generalizing use of the strategy.

Several points must be kept in mind when using evaluation training with culturally and linguistically different students. Since these students may be limited in English proficiency, the monolingual English speaking teacher must increase the amount of demonstration and visual cues and rely less upon verbal descriptions and cues. If available, bilingual assistance from peers or other education personnel may be useful in translating what is discussed in the classroom. This is especially important in order to provide explicit information to students concerning the rationale and value of the strategy. In addition, analogy elaboration of the evaluation strategy may be drawn from the students' cultural and linguistic backgrounds. This reinforces the validity of the students' previous successful learning and increases the ability of the students to make associations which will strengthen their cognitive development.

Evaluation - Applying the Strategy...

Step 1: <u>Analysis</u>

> Teacher—"You must analyze the task to determine what it requires. This includes items such as materials, time, space, or types of actions. What is the expected outcome of the task? What steps must you follow in order to complete the task? Review other completed assignments to determine possible steps you might take to complete this task."

> Student—"What do I need to do to complete

this task, and do I have all
necessary materials and resources?
What should the expected outcome
look like? What steps must I follow
to effectively achieve the expected
outcome?"

Step 2: <u>Strategy Identification</u>

Teacher–"After you have analyzed the task,
you must identify possible
strategies that might be used to
accomplish the task. Think about
strategies you have used in the past
to complete similar tasks. One or
more of these may be necessary to
complete this task."

Student–"What strategies do I know that
might be appropriate for this
particular task? Why might these be
useful in this particular
situation?"

Step 3: <u>Strategy Implementation</u>

Teacher–"Prior to using a selected strategy,
review the steps in that strategy.
Remember that one strategy may be
used in several different situations
and different situations may require
the use of more than one strategy."

Student–"I have selected these strategies
for this task. I will review the
process associated with each
strategy prior to implementation. I
will use these strategies while I
complete this task."

Step 4: <u>Feedback</u>

> Teacher–"You must become aware of how useful it is to use the strategies you have selected. They assist you to complete the task accurately and efficiently. Periodically reflect upon how you are doing and how effective the strategy is for completing the task at hand."

> Student–"How useful is this strategy for this particular task? Is this strategy helping me to accurately and efficiently confront the assigned task? Do I need to use a different strategy?"

Step 5: <u>Elaboration and Generalization</u>

> Teacher–"Think of other previously completed tasks where use of one or more of these strategies would have been beneficial to confronting the tasks. Could you have completed those tasks more efficiently had you used these strategies? Think of other types of tasks or future tasks where you might appropriately use one or more of these strategies."

> Student–"Why were these strategies useful to this particular task? In what other types of situations would the use of these strategies be beneficial?"

Organization

Paris, Newman, and McVey (1982) and Gelzheiser (1984) have demonstrated that recall and retrieval can be enhanced by the use of grouping or cluster strategies. Learning to group or cluster items is an application of the cognitive learning strategy "organization." In organization strategies, students are instructed to follow these steps:

1) Sort the words, items, or information to be recalled into groups sharing some common characteristics;

2) Give these groups distinctive names or labels;

3) Study the items by group, rehearsing the individual and group names;

4) Self-test for recall by group; and,

5) Retrieve item identifications by group (Paris et al., 1982).

As discussed in Section I, some students, and especially those from different cultural and linguistic backgrounds, may need instruction in the process of grouping or the act of categorizing. As noted previously, the way in which students categorize, differentiate, or group items will be largely dependent upon their previous experiences and cultural orientations. Within these considerations, prior to teaching cluster strategies the teacher should demonstrate how to group; how to identify associations, similarities, and differences; and, the range of applicability of this skill. This may be accomplished by having minority students share their existing organization clusters and discuss how similar and different these are to the groupings the students are to learn. For example, the students may be asked to group types of apparel by their function. Similarities and differences in function can be drawn from their own experiences. The same items may be re-grouped based upon factors such as where they are worn on the body, color, or texture. Another example of the

organization cognitive learning strategy is to have
students think about how their homes are organized.
After discussing similarities and differences
between home organizations, the teacher leads
students to discuss the usefulness of organizing
their homes or other items. From these discussions
the analogy is made to organizing thoughts and
memories to enhance retrieval.

Organization - Applying the Strategy...

Step 1: <u>Sorting</u>

> Teacher-"Items can be organized in various
> ways depending upon their function
> and use. Think about how things in
> your home or room are organized and
> what might occur if some pattern
> for sorting and organizing items
> did not exist."

> Student-"I must examine these items and
> identify similar elements or
> patterns within them. I am searching
> for ways to sort and organize the
> items into meaningful clusters with
> shared characteristics."

Step 2: <u>Labeling</u>

> Teacher-"To assist you to remember the
> individual items in your pattern or
> cluster, it helps to give a label to
> the whole group based upon shared
> characteristics."

> Student-"Based upon the patterns that I
> perceive, I will provide a name for
> each of the groups of items I am
> trying to learn."

Step 3: <u>Studying</u>

Teacher—"Examine the items individually and in their groups. Study the whole group and individual items together. This will enable you to more easily remember the group and individual items because you have linked them together."

Student—"I will practice grouping these items. I will examine the individual items in their groups to better remember each item and associated group."

Step 4: <u>Self-Test</u>

Teacher—"While looking at the items say the names of the groups to yourself. Then, without looking at the items, say the names of the groups and the individual items within the groups. Practice this several times until you recall each group name and associated individual items without looking at the items. This will assist you to organize what you are learning and to check to see whether your organization is effective in helping you to learn the items and associated groups."

Student—"I will review the groups and associated items by saying them without looking at the individual items. I will check to see that my organization of the items is helping me to remember the items and groups by saying the names of the groups without looking at the items."

Rehearsal

Rehearsal has also been shown to be an effective cognitive learning strategy. In rehearsal, students are instructed to practice saying each item aloud and by groups of items. As early as 1971, Belmont and Butterfield showed that students with mental retardation made significant gains in recall when taught to rehearse. Rose, Cunick, and Higbee (1983) also documented that verbal rehearsal significantly improved retention and comprehension. The students in this study were trained to use a verbal rehearsal strategy by being instructed to pause after reading a few sentences and talk to themselves about what they were reading. In addition, visual cues were used (i.e., red dots were placed in the margin of the reading passage after every 3 or 4 lines). The students were told that these were "stoplights" which signaled them to stop for a moment and rehearse what they had read since the last "stoplight." Visual cues and visual imagery also have been shown to enhance retention whether in conjunction with verbal rehearsal or as a form of rehearsal themselves.

Rehearsal - Applying the Strategy...

Step 1: <u>Pause</u>

> Teacher-"Learn to stop after each new idea, passage, or element and review it in your mind."

> Student-"What have I just heard, read, or seen? I will mentally review these as I am learning them."

Step 2: <u>Question</u>

> Teacher-"After reviewing the passage,

element, or idea ask questions which
will assist you to remember the
content and the implications of what
it might mean."

Student—"I will ask myself questions such as
who, what, where, when, and why
about what I have just read, heard,
or seen in order to best remember
the information."

Step 3: <u>Visualize</u>

Teacher—"When you stop to review what has
just occurred, make a movie or
picture of the event or idea in your
mind."

Student—"I will generate a mental picture or
movie depicting what I have just
seen, read, or heard."

Step 4: <u>Summarize</u>

Teacher—"When you have finished reading or
listening, summarize to yourself
what has occurred. Organize your
thoughts based upon the answers to
the who, what, where, why, and when
questions. Associate these responses
with the visualizations generated.
Now, when you need to remember this
information rather than going
through all of the steps you need
only recall the summary."

Student—"I will organize my questions,
responses, and visualizations. I
will attempt to remember only the
most important points. I will form a
summary picture and pattern of

questions to help me remember the
essential information."

These discussions conclude with a detailed
description of a combined learning strategies
training process which we have found useful with
minority students identified as learning disabled.
These strategies are presented in Table 4 and were
taught to Hispanic students with learning
disabilities at the beginning of a science unit.
Table 4 identifies 10 specific strategies associated
with one or more of the general cognitive learning
strategy clusters. The Table also illustrates the
visual cues and the instructions which were provided
to the students as these strategies were employed.

The learners were presented with visual cues for
each strategic element. These were placed on index
cards and were simple line drawings illustrative of
the particular cognitive learning strategy. Students
were trained in the purpose and use of these
strategies through short daily discussions between
the teacher and students. Initially, the students
were led through the strategies prior to each new
learning situation. Gradually this was reduced to
daily or weekly "booster shots" and discussions of
the benefits the students were experiencing by using
the strategies. Analogies to the students'
experiences at home or in their previous schools or
communities were used to describe each learning
strategy as discussed above. Cross-cultural learning
experiences were shared which illustrated a
successful use of the strategy and the potential
benefits. If the teacher is unsure whether or not
students are using a particular strategy, the
students may be instructed to talk quietly aloud to
themselves as they complete a task. This will
provide the teacher with information concerning the
cognitive strategies the students are using and the
opportunity to provide feedback to the students.

Maintenance and Generalization

The maintenance and generalization of cognitive strategies are of much concern among educators of students with learning and behavior problems. Mastropieri and Scruggs (1984) noted that generalization of techniques and strategies learned in the special education classroom rarely occurs spontaneously among exceptional students when they return to mainstreamed classes. Generalization and transfer must be taught along with specific learning strategies to maximize their effective utilization and maintenance over time. Mastropieri and Scruggs recommended several instructional strategies to improve generalization. They included:

1. Verbal or written instruction. The teacher reminds the student that he or she has performed this academic or social skill successfully in the special educational setting. The student is also reminded that the same performance is expected in the regular classroom. These are either verbal reminders or notes written directly to the student.

2. Feedback. The teacher provides the student with feedback immediately following performance of the target skill. The teacher also provides verbal feedback immediately after production of a targeted social behavior.

3. Reteaching and positive practice. The teacher reteaches targeted skills in the regular class setting using the same instructional procedures as the special education teacher. Positive practice, similar to reteaching, simply consists of the teacher requiring the student to practice the skill correctly several times. This could be done immediately after reteaching.

Table 4
Instructional Use of Cognitive Learning Strategies

CLUSTERS	STRATEGY	VISUAL CUE	INSTRUCTIONS
Active Processing Coping Rehearsal	Stop and think	STOP	Students are asked to remember when "look before you leap" has been valuable to them. Also discussed are the benefits of reflection.
Active Processing Evaluation Rehearsal	The five W's	W HO HAT HY HERE HEN	Students are led to use these elements in their self-questioning exercises. Also discussed are ways to elaborate upon them.
Analogy Rehearsal	Practice	PRACTICE	The benefits of "practice makes perfect" and rehearsals are discussed. Analogies to previous experiences are elicited.
Active Processing Evaluation	Check your work		The benefits of self-monitoring and evaluating are discussed. Ways that students can assess accurately are discussed.
Coping Evaluation Organization	Break it into smaller parts		Students are shown how to group information into smaller pieces and discuss the benefits of taking smaller bites. Also discussed is how to put things back together.

		generating visual cues or notes as aids in questioning, rehearsing, and organizing information.
Rehearsal		
Analogy Organization	 Organize	The benefits of organizing information are discussed using analogies from students' own experiences. The students think of their minds as houses and how keeping things in particular rooms/places facilitates access.
Active Processing Coping Rehearsal	 Take time/takes time	Students are reminded that learning and development take time. Cultural differences in time use and bio-rhythms are discussed as well the effective use of time.
Analogy Organization	 Look for patterns	The benefits of identifying and using patterns are discussed. Students are shown how to make analogies in using patterns. Patterns learned in students' own languages and cultures are used to illustrate transfer and flexibility.
Analogy Coping	 Think about other things you know about the topic	Students are led to generate questions which will elicit prior knowledge about the topic.

4. <u>Rewards or contracts</u>. The teacher gives the student a direct reward for demonstrating the appropriate skill in the regular class. This reward could take the form of classroom or school privileges, free time, or if necessary, points or tokens which could be exchanged at a later time for something the student desires. Contracts are written agreements between student and teacher specifying a longer term reward and the academic or social skills which must be performed to earn the reward.

5. <u>Enlisting peer cooperation</u>. In this last and most time-consuming intervention, the teacher enlists the aid of other students in the class to help the mainstreamed student. The teacher pairs the student with a peer who at specified times tutors the student in the targeted skill area.

These authors also noted that the cooperation of the special educator and the regular classroom teacher is crucial to the success of these strategies. The topic of collaboration among special and regular educators concerning cognitive learning strategies usage in mainstream settings in discussed in Section III.

SECTION III
ACCOMMODATING COGNITIVE AND LEARNING STYLES IN THE MAINSTREAM

Effective program implementation for minority handicapped students also includes appropriate considerations and accommodations made when education occurs in non-special education classrooms (e.g., ESL classes, bilingual education, regular education). The current educational placement for many handicapped learners (including minority handicapped) is education in regular classes and special classes. Both positive and potentially negative aspects associated with this type of placement are well documented in the literature (Dunn, 1968; Gearheart & Weishahn, 1984; Polloway, Payne, Patton, & Payne, 1985; Reynolds & Birch, 1982). In addition, most practicing teachers have experiences related to positive and negative issues surrounding education in regular and special classes. If cognitive learning strategy development is to succeed adequately, teachers in both regular and special education classrooms must provide opportunity for the practice and use of the strategies.

One of the many responsibilities of special educators is to work with regular class teachers concerning the mainstreaming of exceptional students (Friend, 1985; McClellan & Wheatley, 1985). Exceptional minority students may also be mainstreamed into bilingual or ESL classrooms. The special educator's responsibilities include familiarizing other educators with issues such as those which pertain to the effect of handicapping conditions upon first and second language development, the interaction between minority concerns and handicapping conditions, as well as various educational program factors. This consultation may be completed as part of the special educator's participation in a child study team at the prereferral level as well as after special education program placement.

The discussion in this Section centers on various techniques and strategies that may be employed by special educators concerning the education of minority handicapped students, when working with other classroom teachers. The information provided in this Section is presented relative to assisting other educators to understand and facilitate student use of cognitive learning strategies as discussed in the previous sections. However, the information presented is applicable for assisting teachers in various areas of education. For additional information about other related issues pertaining to minority and handicapped learners not specifically addressed in this book, the reader is referred to Baca and Cervantes (1984) and Hoover and Collier (1986).

Program Collaboration

Cooperation and collaboration between special and regular educators must occur in order to ensure success with each individual program for minority handicapped learners. The previous sections of this book have addressed one important aspect of an educational program for these special learners (i.e., cognitive learning strategy development). Program collaboration in this area of development includes attention to several aspects of a student's program. Special, regular, and bilingual/ESL educators must be familiar with various aspects of cognitive and learning style; specific strategies that may be used to develop cognitive and learning skills; specific strategies most effective for individual minority handicapped learners; and, how cognitive learning strategies may be appropriately integrated into programs in regular and special education classrooms.

Program collaboration from both the special educator's and regular educator's perspectives involves an on-going exchange of knowledge, skills, and expertise. Specifically, issues discussed in the previous sections must be addressed by educators to ensure appropriate education for each minority student. Many teachers in regular education classrooms are very willing to address specific needs of minority handicapped learners, provided they feel competent with their own skills and abilities. The special educator can provide valuable support and assistance to regular and bilingual/ESL classroom teachers in efforts to provide consistent education relative to cognitive learning strategy development and use.

Figure 2 illustrates one process that may be followed by special and regular educators to ensure effective program collaboration. The process associated with this model reflects the primary goal of ensuring consistent implementation of cognitive learning strategy development and usage in all class settings. The elements within the model are classified into three stages:

1. Development Stage
2. Implementation Stage
3. Evaluation Stage

Each of these is discussed briefly.

Development Stage

Strategies used frequently and regularly by the student in a special education classroom may also be used effectively in other classes, provided the student is proficient in the use of the strategy. During the Development Stage, the special educator must identify specific cognitive learning strategies employed by the learner in the special education classroom. Once identified, the curriculum followed outside of the special education setting is analyzed in efforts to identify specific content, strategies, and materials used. Specifically, the student-curriculum match (i.e., compatibility between teacher or curricular expectations and student abilities) must be determined.

Smith, Neisworth, and Greer (1978) discussed three general areas to address as one analyzes a potential student and curriculum match. They include the Task, Structure, and Reward elements. The Task dimension focuses on the student's ability to perform within the curriculum and teacher expectations. Some learners will function at low levels of performance while others perform at higher levels. Students functioning at lower task levels require assignments that are highly structured and directed as appropriate attention and response patterns are being developed. Students functioning at higher performance levels are capable of completing assignments that use less teacher direction and foster creativity and originality on the part of the students. Since performance and ability levels will vary across subject areas, assignments must also vary to meet individual task levels of different students.

The Structure element refers to the classroom groupings (i.e., one-one, group work, independent work). Similar to the previous dimension, minority handicapped students will vary in their structure or grouping needs. Some students may require a specific type of grouping or independent structure while others may be more flexible and capable in dealing with various grouping situations. In reference to cognitive learning strategies, these may assist students to work more effectively within different grouping structures. Once student needs and abilities concerning grouping structures in the mainstream class have been determined, the special educator should identify those cognitive learning strategies in the student's repertoire that may assist in meeting structure demands. As emphasized previously, the overall goal is to facilitate more effective learning within various structures through use of cognitive learning skills to minimize academic or behavior problems.

The Reward element refers to the types of rewards the student requires as educational tasks are completed. These may vary from highly tangible (e.g., points, tokens) to intangible rewards such as personal satisfaction in one's progress. Similar to the other dimensions, the reward levels of students will vary, and the use of cognitive learning strategies may assist students to require less

Figure 2
Model for Cognitive Learning Strategies Program Collaboration

| Identify cognitive strategies student has acquired | → | Determine discrepancies in student-curriculum match | → | Identify strategies in student's repertoire to address discrepancies | → | Develop plan to implement program in regular class |

DEVELOPMENT STAGE

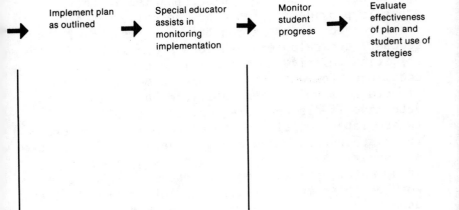

IMPLEMENTATION
STAGE

EVALUATION
STAGE

external and more intrinsic forms of rewards.

One major goal for determining the student-curriculum match is to identify cognitive learning strategies that may be used appropriately and effectively by the student in the regular class to address discrepancies between student abilities and teacher/curriculum expectations relative to task, structure, and reward needs. A guide to follow for identifying possible discrepancies in these areas is provided in Table 5. The guide has been completed for illustration purposes. As shown, the teacher/curriculum expectations along with student abilities relative to a specific assignment are documented for each of the three dimensions. The expectations and student abilities are compared to determine if discrepancies exist. The guide should be completed jointly by the cooperating educators for a student for each specific assignment where use of cognitive learning strategies is desired (e.g., group math, spelling test, independent reading or workbook page completion). This information is then used to develop a plan for student use of cognitive learning strategies in the regular class to facilitate intrinsic motivation and independent learning.

The information in Table 6 provides a guide to document and outline a program for student use of cognitive learning strategies in the regular class. As shown, the discrepancies between the teacher/curriculum expectations and student abilities associated with the task, structure, and reward dimensions are documented. This information is obtained from the guide presented in Table 5. Based upon these discrepancies, a specific objective pertaining to the subject area and assignment is outlined. The objective should assist to reduce or eliminate discrepancies in one or more of the three dimensions. Once the objective for reducing the discrepancy is outlined, specific cognitive learning strategies that the student will use to achieve this objective are documented. Thus, the desired goal will address some discrepancy associated within the

Table 5
Guide for Determining Student-Curriculum Match

Name: Tony

Assignment: Participate in small reading group discussions

Grade: 5   Date: 11/87

* *

Dimension	Teacher/Curriculum Expectations	Student Ability	Discrepancy
TASK	Draw conclusions and make inferences after silently reading a story written at Tony's instructional level in English.	Experiences difficulty recalling story content after silent reading.	Student lacks sufficient memory or attention skills to complete task.
STRUCTURE	Small group work	Capable of working in small group situations especially when one or two other Hispanic students are included.	None
REWARD	Verbal recognition and praise to reward efforts. Praise is provided in both English and Spanish.	Responds generally well to verbal praise especially when Spanish is used.	None

61

Table 6
Plan for Program Implementation

Name: __Tony_____   Date: __11/87___

Subject:__Reading_____

Assignment:__Small group discussions__

* *

1. Discrepancy

   Task Level- Tony lacks sufficient memory or attention
                skills to complete reading task.
   Structure Level- None

   Reward Level- None

2. Objective(s)
   Increase Tony's ability to recall information and provide
   correct responses during small reading group discussions.

3. Cognitive Learning Strategy(s)
   Active Processing-Self-question techniques.

4. Minimum Duration of Program
   Three school weeks.

5. Specific Instructions for Implementing Program
   Teacher will remind Tony to use self-question techniques
   prior to each small reading group activity where silent
   reading is necessary. Self-generated questions may be in
   English or Spanish. Self-questioning techniques are
   to be reviewed daily with Tony in both English and
   Spanish.

6. Evaluation Procedures and Program Monitoring
   Using a simple checklist, the teacher will record the
   number of correct responses Tony makes during each
   small reading group activity. Prompting and verbal
   praise will be used to encourage and reward Tony's use
   of Active Processing strategies as well as correct
   answers provided by Tony.

task, structure, or reward dimension as one or more learning style aspects are addressed through student use of cognitive learning strategies. The plan also provides an opportunity to delineate how the program will be implemented, the minimum length of time it will run, and the basis for evaluation of the plan and objective. The program plan has been completed for illustration purposes.

Implementation Stage

Once the plan for including the use of specific cognitive learning strategies in the regular class has been developed and the teacher is familiar with the strategies that the student will use, the plan is implemented. During the implementation stage, the regular classroom teacher is responsible for ensuring that the student has opportunities to use the skills outlined in the plan as well as general monitoring of the program. Where possible, the special educator should assist the regular or bilingual/ESL classroom teacher in the implementation of the program, and support the program in the special education classroom. The special educator should also begin to assist with the monitoring of the program as it is implemented. The program should continue for the specified amount of time, and once the plan is implemented, the final stage in this process begins.

Evaluation Stage

The evaluation component of this model emphasizes evaluating both the plan for including cognitive learning strategies use in the classroom as well as the effects upon the desired objective. The specific plan for evaluating the effects upon the desired outcome is documented in the guide described in Table 6. Special educators should monitor student use of the strategies by discussing this with the student on a daily basis. A simple self-monitoring checklist could be developed and completed by the student each time he or she employs the desired skill. Or, if the plan outlines use of a skill readily observable by the regular classroom teacher, the teacher might complete a simple checklist indicating observed use of the desired skill on a daily basis. On-going monitoring of the program by special and regular educators must occur along with the summative evaluation of the effects upon the desired goal (e.g., improved spelling test scores, increased attention during small group, completed assignments).

In addition to the evaluation of the effects of specific cognitive learning strategy use, the plan for implementing the program should also be evaluated. This may be accomplished by discussing the program with the classroom teacher(s) on a regular basis to identify and resolve existing problems. Although minor program changes can be made, major changes should be avoided until the program has been completed for the specified minimum amount of time. Careful and cooperative planning during the development stage will assist to minimize the need for major program changes. Upon completion of the program, all teachers involved should consult and determine the effects of the student use of the specific cognitive learning strategy(s) on the desired objective as well as the method for implementing the program, and decide upon the next course of action based upon these results.

As indicated at the beginning of this discussion, Figure 2 outlined a three stage model that may be followed when developing, implementing, and evaluating a cognitive learning strategy program in the regular class. Modifications to this model may be easily incorporated into the total process and should be made as student needs and abilities dictate. However, this model outlines a general approach that may be followed along with important considerations when attempting to improve independent learning in the regular classroom.

Although several important features of this model have been outlined and discussed, one other important component must also be addressed (i.e., the interaction between regular and special educators). The best laid plans may have little chance to succeed if the special educator is not sensitive to the needs of the other classroom teachers. The special educator's skills to assist other educators in the development, implementation, and evaluation stages of a cognitive learning strategy program in regular classes must also be addressed. The interpersonal and consulting skills employed by the special educator will, to a great extent, relate directly to the success or failure of the cognitive learning strategy program. In essence, how the special educator goes about dealing and working with other educators is equally as important as the quality of information shared.

Consultant Skills for Effective Collaboration

One of the greatest challenges a special education teacher must confront is that of working effectively with other educators to ensure appropriate programming in the mainstream setting. Within the current structure of mainstreaming, special educators are continually faced with the dilemma of providing consistent education to special learners in and out of special class settings. This also applies to the development and use of cognitive learning strategies in these settings. To ensure the best possible success in program collaborative endeavors, the special educator should be familiar with various important issues and recognize and possess several consulting skills or competencies. Numerous issues and competencies associated with effective consultation and program collaboration have been identified and investigated (Harris & Schutz, 1986; Hoover, Blasi, Geiger, Ritter, & Sileo, 1986; Idol-Maestas & Ritter, 1985; Lippitt & Lippitt, 1978). These include knowledge and skills related to these general areas:

1 - Teaching and Behavior Management Strategies
2 - Curriculum Adaptation
3 - Facilitating Change
4 - School and District Resources and Policies
5 - Assessment and Referral Procedures
6 - Effective Communication
7 - Teacher Concerns

It is beyond the scope of this book to address each of these important skills and we have, therefore, limited our discussions at this time to three of these general areas which are especially relevant to our purpose: 1) Teacher Concerns; 2) Facilitating Change; and, 3) Communication and Interpersonal Relationship Skills. However, in reference to the issues surrounding school and district resources and policies, the special educator must be familiar with these prior to attempting any collaborative programs. This information is important when considering the development, implementation, and evaluation of a cognitive learning strategy program outside the special education class. For additional information about curricular adaptations and teaching and behavior management strategies relative to minority handicapped students, the reader is referred to Baca and Cervantes (1984) and Hoover and Collier (1986). The reader is also referred to McLoughlin and Lewis (1986) and Salvia and Ysseldyke (1985) for information about the assessment and referral of special learners and to Idol, Paolucci-Whitcomb, and Nevin (1986) for additional information about consultation.

Teacher Concerns

Hallahan and Kauffman (1986) and Heron and Harris (1987) suggested several teacher concerns and problems associated with the education of handicapped students in regular classes. These included:

1. The assumption that mainstreaming will be readily accepted by regular educators;

2. Lack of teacher preparation to work with handicapped students in the regular class;

3. Inconsistent or non-existent special education support services to facilitate effective mainstreaming;

4. Regular educators' concern with accountability for the educational progress of handicapped students in their classes; and,

5. Lack of knowledge about and participation in the instructional planning and implementing of a program for the handicapped.

These and similar concerns and problems represent some of the major issues confronting the special educator as program collaboration is attempted. If program collaboration is to succeed, these problems and concerns must be addressed and carefully considered by the special educator. Since the extent to which these concerns exist will vary from school to school and classroom to classroom, the special educator must make judgments on a "situation-specific" basis and adjust the emphasis and direction of the program collaboration accordingly. The special educator must be familiar with district or school policies concerning accountability, support services, and programming for the handicapped and minorities. The concerns of classroom teachers must be identified and considered from the onset of program collaboration. As teacher concerns are minimized and dealt with and as teachers acquire additional knowledge about minority handicapped students, programs for student development and use of cognitive learning strategies have a greater chance to succeed.

Facilitating Change

In many situations, the introduction of a cognitive learning strategies program in the regular classroom requires that the teacher change one or more aspects within the classroom. This includes potentially changing seating arrangements, assignments, teaching strategies, groupings, reward structures, or classroom rules. To a great extent the success or failure of a program implemented in the regular or bilingual/ESL class rests upon how well the special educator assists the classroom teacher in dealing with and implementing changes that may be necessary as a result of the cognitive learning strategy program.

The information in Table 7 outlines several factors associated with creating and implementing effective change. The Table was derived from information found in Doll (1978) and is applied specifically to special and regular education program collaboration. Should change in either the curriculum implementation process or in specific teacher behaviors or practices be required, adhering to these principles may assist in the successful planning and implementing of a cognitive learning strategies program in the non-special education classrooms. As shown, various factors contribute to effective change. The predominant theme, however, emphasizes cooperative planning within a problem-solving structure where respect for each teacher's needs (related to change) prevails. Special educators should consider these factors as program collaboration with regular and bilingual/ESL educators occurs.

In addition to knowledge about these factors associated with change, special educators must also be familiar with a process associated with change. Doll (1978) outlined one process associated with effective change as teachers engage in new patterns of behavior. The process includes several steps that one should follow as change is implemented. The individual involved in the change must be:

Table 7
Critical Factors Associated with Effective Change

Success levels associated with change improve as the:

1. Teachers conducting the change work on problems they perceive as important to address;

2. Direction for change is determined cooperatively by the regular class and special education teachers;

3. Teachers acquire experience related to the issues or tasks that they are changing;

4. Number of factors associated with the change are kept to a minimum;

5. Channels of communication between educators are kept open and honest;

6. Planning for change is completed jointly by those involved;

7. Problem-solving sessions are kept task-oriented and specific to issues necessary to create the change;

8. Special and regular educators respect each other's capacities for change (i.e., some people change more rapidly or more slowly than others).

1 - Made aware of the possibility of change;

2 - Interested in changing;

3 - Provided time to consider the potential worth
    of the proposed change; and,

4 - Allowed to execute the change on a small,
    specific scale prior to the full implementation
    of the proposed change.

The chances for success with the proposed change will improve greatly if the teacher is able to deal successfully with each of these steps. Special educators should ensure that each of these steps is addressed as program collaboration occurs. Referring to our model for program collaboration, the elements and steps related to change should be addressed initially in the Development Stage and continually emphasized through the Implementation and Evaluation Stages.

Communication and Interpersonal Relationship Skills

As the special educator considers the factors and processes associated with change and works with the regular and bilingual/ESL classroom teachers through the model for program collaboration, various qualities and skills will assist in building and maintaining necessary communication and interpersonal relationships associated with collaboration. Harris and Schutz (1986), Lippitt and Lippitt (1978), and Stewart (1986) have identified several abilities and qualities important in the communication and interpersonal relationship process associated with consulting. These authors wrote that effective consultants or helpers:

1 - Know their own needs and limits of ability;

2 - Clarify their own expectations;

3 - Convey respect, empathy, and understanding toward others;

4 - Establish and maintain effective rapport;

5 - Are effective and careful listeners;

6 - Avoid providing solutions until all pertinent information has been gathered;

7 - Are supportive of others' efforts and needs;

8 - Are nonjudgmental and tolerant towards others;

9 - Are informed and knowledgeable about the specific issues addressed in the program collaboration; and,

10 - Gradually and systematically introduce their knowledge and skills to the regular educators in an objective and non-threatening manner.

These qualities are not presented in any rank order of importance and the list is not intended to include every quality. Rather, some of the more important qualities are summarized, recognizing that all are important to ensure success with program collaboration. The use of cognitive learning strategies by minority handicapped students in all class settings is essential to ensure generalization of learning as well as success in each type of setting. Familiarity with factors associated with change and the development of the "consultant qualities" will assist in the success of collaboration as teacher concerns and student learning needs are addressed through use of cognitive learning strategies in both special and regular education settings.

Summary

Cognitive learning strategies for minority handicapped students has explored four important areas related to the education of minority students who are handicapped. They are: 1) cognitive styles; 2) learning styles; 3) cognitive learning strategy clusters; and, 4) program collaboration to facilitate effective use of cognitive learning strategies in both special education and mainstreamed classrooms. Seven important cognitive styles were explored along with associated learning styles. Six cognitive learning strategies were also discussed in detail. Numerous examples were provided to illustrate proper use of the cognitive learning strategy clusters addressed in this book. The proper use of the cognitive learning strategy clusters presented in this book will assist students to become more independent learners. Through the identification of specific learning styles of students, the teacher is best able to plan and implement instruction which provides learners with opportunities to acquire information which is compatible with their own individual needs. It is the authors' hope that the contents of this book encourage both special and regular educators to address cognitive learning strategies development and usage in their classes for minority students who are handicapped.

References

Adler, P. S. (1975). The transitional experience: An alternative view of culture shock. Journal of Humanistic Psychology, 15, 13-23.

Alley, G., & Deshler, D. (1979). Teaching the learning disabled adolescent: Strategies and methods. Denver: Love Publishing.

Baca, L. M., & Cervantes, H. T. (1984). The bilingual special education interface. St. Louis: Times Mirror/Mosby.

Belmont, J. M., & Butterfield, E. C. (1971). Learning strategies as determinants of memory deficiencies. Cognitive Psychology, 2, 411-420.

Ben-Zeev, S. (1977). The influence of bilingualism on cognitive strategy and cognitive development. Child Development, 48, 1009-1018.

Blumenthal, A. L. (1977). The Process of cognition. Englewood Cliffs, NJ: Prentice-Hall.

Brown, A. L. (1980). Metacognitive development and reading. In R. J. Spiro, B. B. Bruce, & W. F. Brewer (Eds.), Theoretical issues in reading comprehension. (pp. 453-481). Hillsdale, NJ: Earlbaum.

Casson, R. (1981). Language, culture, and cognition. New York, NY: Macmillan Publishing.

Cawley, J. F. (Ed.). (1985). Cognitive strategies and mathematics for the learning disabled. Rockville, MD: Aspen Publishers, Inc.

Collier, C. (1985). A comparison of acculturation and education characteristics of referred and nonreferred culturally and linguistically different children. (Doctoral dissertation,

University of Colorado, Boulder, 1985).
Dissertation Abstracts International, 46, 2993A.

Collier, C. (1984). Bilingual special education
curriculum development. In L. M. Baca and H.
Cervantes (Eds.), The bilingual special education
interface. (pp. 233-268). Columbus: Merrill
Publishing.

Cornett, C. E. (1983). What you should know about
teaching and styles. Bloomington, IN: Phi Delta
Kappa Educational Foundation.

Delpit, L. (1986). Comprehending cross-culturally.
Education Exchange, 8, 1-2. (College of Human and
Rural Development Newsletter, University of
Alaska).

Doll, R. C. (1978). Curriculum improvement: Decision
making and process. Boston: Allyn and Bacon, Inc.

Dudley-Marling, C. C., Sinder, V., & Tarver, S. G.
(1982). Locus of control and learning
disabilities: A review and discussion. Perceptual
and Motor Skills, 54, 503-514.

Dunn, L. M. (1968). Special education for the mildly
handicapped - Is much of it justifiable?
Exceptional Children, 35, 5-22.

Dyal, J. A. (1984). Cross-cultural research with the
locus of control construct. In H. M. Lefcourt
(Ed.), Research with the locus of control
construct (Vol. 3, pp. 209-305). New York:
Academic Press, Inc.

Englert, C. S., Hiebert, E. H., & Stewart, S. R.
(1985). Spelling unfamiliar words by an analogy
strategy. Journal of Special Education, 19,
291-306.

Epstein, H. T. (1978). Growth spurts during brain development: Implications for educational policy and practice. In J. Chall and A. Mirsky (Eds.), Education and the brain. (pp. 343-370). Chicago: University of Chicago Press.

Feldman, C., & Shen, M. (1971). Some language-related cognitive advantages of bilingual five-year-olds. The Journal of Genetic Psychology, 118, 235-244.

Feuerstein, R. (1979). Instrumental environment: An intervention program for cognitive modifiability. Baltimore: University Park Press.

Friend, M. (1985). Training special educators to be consultants: Considerations for developing programs. Teacher Education and Special Education, 8, 115-120.

Gardner, R. W. (1953). Cognitive styles in categorizing behavior. Journal of Personality, 22, 214-233.

Gardner, R. W., Jackson, D. N., & Messick, S. J. (1960). Personality organization in cognitive controls and intellectual abilities. Psychological Issues, 2, 1-149.

Gearheart, B. R., DeRuiter, J. A., & Sileo, T. W. (1986). Teaching mildly and moderately handicapped students. Englewood Cliffs: Prentice-Hall, Inc.

Gearheart, B. R., and Weishahn, M. W. (1984). The exceptional student in the regular classroom. St. Louis: Times Mirror/Mosby.

Gelzheiser, L. M. (1984). Generalization from categorical memory tasks to prose by learning disabled adolescents. Journal of Educational Psychology, 76, 1128-1138.

Goodenough, W. H. (1957). Cultural anthropology and linguistics. In P. Garvin (Ed.), Report of the 7th annual meeting on linguistics and language study. Washington, D.C.: Georgetown University Monograph Series on Language and Linguistics (No. 9).

Hallahan, D. P., & Kauffman, J. M. (1986). Exceptional children: Introduction to special education. Englewood Cliffs: Prentice-Hall, Inc.

Harris, W. J., & Schutz, P. N. B. (1986). The special education resource program: Rationale and implementation. Columbus: Merrill Publishing.

Heron, T. E., & Harris, K. C. (1987). The educational consultant - Helping professionals, parents, and mainstreamed students. Austin, TX: Pro-Ed.

Hoover, J. J., Blasi, J., Geiger, W., Ritter, S., & Sileo, T. W. (1986). Undergraduate special education teacher training programs in comprehensive and noncomprehensive schools: Phase I. Teacher Education and Special Education, 9, 202-209.

Hoover, J. J., & Collier, C. (1986). Classroom management through curricular adaptations: Educating minority handicapped students. Lindale, TX: Hamilton Publications.

Ianco-Worral, A. D. (1972). Bilingualism and cognitive development. Child Development, 43, 1390-1400.

Idol, L., Paolucci-Whitcomb, P., & Nevin, A. (1986). Collaborative consultation. Rockville, MD: Aspen Publishers, Inc.

Idol-Maestas, L., & Ritter, S. (1985). A follow-up study of resource/consulting teachers: Factors that facilitate and inhibit teacher consultation. Teacher Education and Special Education, 8, 121-131.

Juffer, K. A. (1983). Culture shock: A theoretical framework for understanding adaptation. In J. Bransford (Ed.), Monograph Series: BUENO Center for Multicultural Education, 4, 136-149.

Keogh, B. K. (1977). Research on cognitive styles. In R. Kneedler and S. Tarver (Eds.), Changing perspectives in special education. Columbus: Charles E. Merrill.

Keogh, B. K. (1973). Perceptual and cognitive styles: Implications for special education. In L. Mann and D. Sabatino (Eds.), The first review of special education. Philadelphia, PA: JSE Press.

Kurtz, B. E., & Borkowski, J. G. (1984). Children's metacognition: Exploring relations among knowledge, process, and motivational variables. Journal of Experimental Child Psychology, 37, 335-354.

Lippitt, G., and Lippitt, R. (1978). The consulting process in action. La Jolla, CA: University Associates, Inc.

Mann, L., & Sabatino, D. A. (1985). Foundations of cognitive process in remedial and special education. Rockville, MD: Aspen Publishers, Inc.

Mastropieri, M. A., & Scruggs, T. E. (1984). Generalization: Five effective strategies. Academic Therapy, 19, 427-431.

McClellan, E., & Wheatley, W. (1985). Project RETOOL: Collaborative consultation training for post-doctoral leadership personnel. Teacher Education and Special Education, 8, 159-163.

McLoughlin, J. A., & Lewis, R. B. (1986). Assessing special students. Columbus: Merrill Publishing.

Meichenbaum, D., & Goodman, J. (1971). Training impulsive children to talk to themselves: A means of developing self-control. Journal of Abnormal Psychology, 77, 115-126.

Miller, G. E. (1985). The effects of general and specific self-instruction training on children's comprehension monitoring performances during reading. Reading Research Quarterly, 20, 616-628.

Padilla, A. (1980). Acculturation: Theory, models, and some new findings. American Association for the Advancement of Science Symposium Series (No. 39). Boulder: Westview Press.

Palincsar, A. S. (1986). Metacognitive strategy instruction. Exceptional Children, 53, 118-125.

Palincsar, A. S., & Brown, A. L. (1987). Enhancing instructional time through attention to metacognition. Journal of Learning Disabilities, 20, 66-75.

Paris, S. G., Newman, R., & McVey, K. (1982). Learning the functional significance of mnemonic actions: A microgenetic study of strategy acquisition. Journal of Experimental Child Psychology, 34, 490-509.

Peck, R. F., Hughes, R., Breeding, J., & Payne, G. C. (1980). Cross-cultural study of adaptative behaviors in the classroom. Paper presented at the Southwest Psychological Association conference in Oklahoma City, Oklahoma.

Polloway, E. A., Payne, J. S., Patton, J. R., & Payne, R. A. (1985). <u>Strategies for teaching retarded and special needs learners</u>. Columbus: Merrill Publishing.

Pressley, M., Borkowski, J. G., & O'Sullivan, J. T. (1984). Memory strategy instruction is made of this: Metamemory and durable strategy use. <u>Educational Psychologist</u>, <u>19</u>, 94-107.

Ramirez, M., & Castaneda, A. (1974). <u>Cultural democracy: Bicognitive development and education</u>. New York: Academic Press, Inc.

Ramirez, M., Castaneda, A., & Herold, P. L. (1974). The relationship of acculturation to cognitive style among mexican americans. <u>Journal of Cross-Cultural Psychology</u>, <u>5</u>, 424-433.

Reynolds, M. C., & Birch, J. W. (1982). <u>Teaching exceptional children in all America's schools</u>. Reston, VA: The Council for Exceptional Children.

Rose, M. C., Cunick, B. P., & Higbee, K. L. (1983). Verbal rehearsal and visual imagery: Mnemonic aids for learning disabled children. <u>Journal of Learning Disabilities</u>, <u>16</u>, 352-354.

Salvia, J., & Ysseldyke, J. E. (1985). <u>Assessment in special and remedial education</u>. Boston: Houghton Mifflin.

Schumaker, J., Deshler, D., Alley, G., Warner, M., & Denton, P. (1984). Multipass: A learning strategy for improving reading comprehension. <u>Learning Disability Quarterly</u>, <u>5</u>, 295-304.

Sheinker, J., & Sheinker, A. (1983). <u>Study strategies: A metacognitive approach</u>. Rock Springs, Wyo: White Mountain Publishing.

Slife, B. D., Weiss, J., & Bell, T. (1985). Separability of metacognition and cognition: Problem solving in learning disabled and regular students. Journal of Educational Psychology, 77, 437-445.

Smith, R. M., Neisworth, J. T., & Greer, J. G. (1978). Evaluating educational environments. Columbus: Charles E. Merrill.

Stewart, J. C. (1986). Counseling parents of exceptional children. Columbus: Merrill Publishing.

Stone, C. A., & Wertsch, J. V. (1984). A social interactional analysis of learning disabilities remediation. Journal of Learning Disabilities, 17, 194-198.

Wong, B. Y. L. (1985). Self-questioning instructional research: A review. Review of Educational Research, 55, 227-268.

Wong, B. Y. L., & Jones, W. (1982). Increasing metacomprehension in learning disabled and normally achieving students through self-questioning training. Learning Disability Quarterly, 5, 228-238.

About the Authors

Catherine Collier received her Ph.D. in 1985 from the University of Colorado, Boulder specializing in Multicultural/Special Education. She has taught exceptional Native American students in grades K-12 and developed and administered programs for Navajo students. Dr. Collier has also developed and administered several teacher training programs in bilingual and special education. She has authored or co-authored several chapters, monographs, and articles in the area of education for culturally and linguistically different exceptional learners, including the book titled "Classroom management through curricular adaptations: Educating minority handicapped students." She is currently Assistant Professor, Adjunct, at the University of Colorado, Boulder, and is Director of the Bilingual Special Education Curriculum Training (BISECT) Project.

John J. Hoover received his Ph.D. in 1983 from the University of Colorado, Boulder specializing in Curriculum/Special Education. He has taught culturally and linguistically different exceptional learners in public and alternative educational settings in grades K-12. Dr. Hoover has also served as an educational consultant to regular class teachers concerning the education of special learners in mainstreamed settings. He has completed numerous evaluations of bilingual and bilingual special education programs at the K-12 and post-secondary levels of education. He has numerous publications in educational journals, including chapters in textbooks discussing study skills education for exceptional learners. He is currently employed as an Assistant Professor of Special Education at the University of Texas, Tyler.